Wheels, Wings, and Water

Aircraft

Lola M. Schaefer

Heinemann Library
Chicago, Illinois

© 2003 Heinemann Library
a division of Reed Elsevier Inc.
Chicago, Illinois

Customer Service 888-454-2279
Visit our website at www.heinemannlibrary.com

Designed by Sue Emerson, Heinemann Library; Page layout by Que-Net Media
Printed and bound in the United States by Lake Book Manufacturing, Inc.
Photo research by Amor Montes De Oca

07 06 05 04 03
10 9 8 7 6 5 4 3 2 1

Library of Congress Cataloging-in-Publication Data
Schaefer, Lola M., 1950-
  Aircraft / Lola M. Schaefer.
      v. cm. — (Wheels, wings, and water)
Includes index.
Contents: What are aircraft? – What do aircraft look like? – What are aircraft made of? – How did aircraft look long ago? – What is an airplane? – What is a jet? – What is a helicopter? – What is a blimp? – What are some special aircraft? – Quiz – Picture glossary.
  ISBN 1-4034-0884-X (HC), 1-4034-3616-9 (Pbk.)
  1. Airplanes—Juvenile literature. [1. Airplanes.] I. Title. II. Series.
TL547.S3323 2003
  629.133'3—dc21

2002014719

Acknowledgments
The author and publishers are grateful to the following for permission to reproduce copyright material:
p. 4 Charles O'Rear/Corbis; pp. 5, 17 Jeffrey Howe/Visuals Unlimited; p. 6 A&E Morris/Visuals Unlimited; p. 7 Norman Owen Tomalin/Bruce Coleman, Inc.; p. 8 Swartzell/Visuals Unlimited; p. 9 Patrick Bennett/Corbis; p. 10 Bettmann/Corbis; p. 11 Museum of Flight/Corbis; p. 12 Matt Bradley/Bruce Coleman, Inc.; p. 13 Jeffrey Greenberg/Visuals Unlimited; p. 14 Bruce Berg/Visuals Unlimited; pp. 15, 22, 24 Philip Wallick/Corbis; p. 16 Arthur Morris/Visuals Unlimited; p. 18 Richard Hamilton Smith/Corbis; p. 19 Carl & Ann Purcell/Corbis; p. 20 Richard T. Nowitz/Corbis; p. 21 Ian & Karen Stewart/Bruce Coleman, Inc.; p. 23 row 1 (L-R) Norman Owen Tomalin/Bruce Coleman, Inc., Ian & Karen Stewart/Bruce Coleman, Inc., Richard T. Nowitz/Corbis; row 2 (L-R) Richard Hamilton Smith/Corbis, Jeffrey Howe/Visuals Unlimited, Charles O'Rear/Corbis; row 3 (L-R) Bruce Berg/Visuals Unlimited, Richard T. Nowitz/Corbis, Ian & Karen Stewart/Bruce Coleman, Inc., Richard Hamilton Smith/Corbis; back cover (L-R) Ian & Karen Stewart/Bruce Coleman, Inc., Richard Hamilton Smith/Corbis

Cover photograph by Matt Bradley/Bruce Coleman, Inc.

Every effort has been made to contact copyright holders of any material reproduced in this book. Any omissions will be rectified in subsequent printings if notice is given to the publisher.

Special thanks to our advisory panel for their help in the preparation of this book:

Alice Bethke, Library Consultant
Palo Alto, CA

Eileen Day, Preschool Teacher
Chicago, IL

Kathleen Gilbert,
Second Grade Teacher
Round Rock, TX

Sandra Gilbert,
Library Media Specialist
Fiest Elementary School
Houston, TX

Jan Gobeille,
Kindergarten Teacher
Garfield Elementary
Oakland, CA

Angela Leeper,
Educational Consultant
North Carolina Department
of Public Instruction
Wake Forest, NC

Some words are shown in bold, **like this.**
You can find them in the picture glossary on page 23.

Contents

What Are Aircraft?

Aircraft are **vehicles** that fly.

They carry people or things in the air.

propeller

engine

Engines and **propellers** make some aircraft fly.

Some aircraft use hot air, gas, or wind to move.

5

What Do Aircraft Look Like?

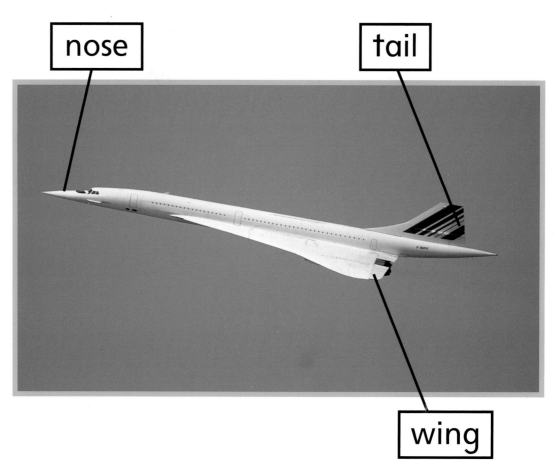

nose

tail

wing

Most aircraft have two wings,
a tail, and a nose.

This airplane looks like a big bird!

blades

Some aircraft do not have wings.

This helicopter has **blades** instead.

What Are Aircraft Made Of?

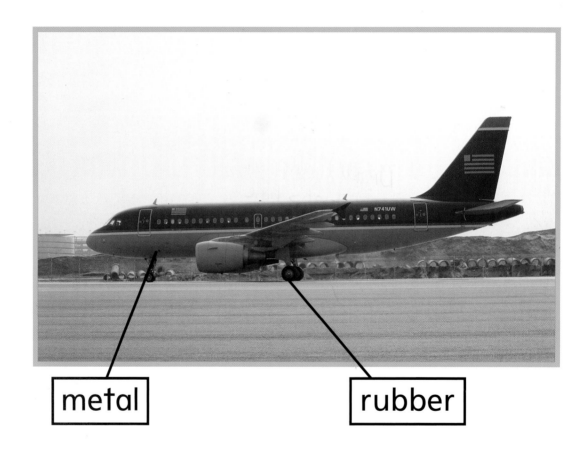

metal

rubber

The outsides of most aircraft are metal.

Tires are made of rubber.

plastic

cloth

The seats in most aircraft are cloth.

Some parts are made of plastic.

How Did Aircraft Look Long Ago?

The first aircraft were made of wood, cloth, and wire.

People who flew them sat on poles.

Then, airplanes were made of metal.

They had windows and doors.

What Is an Airplane?

propeller

An airplane is an aircraft with wings.

Some airplanes are very small.

Airplanes can be big, too.

They can carry many people.

What Is a Jet?

engine

A jet plane looks like an airplane without **propellers.**

A jet's **engines** are stronger than propellers.

Jets fly higher than airplanes.

They are faster, too!

What Is a Helicopter?

blades

Helicopters are aircraft with **blades** instead of **propellers**.

An **engine** turns the blades.

Helicopters can fly up, down,
or sideways.

They can even fly in one place.

What Is a Blimp?

A **blimp** is a large balloon filled with a light gas.

The gas lifts the blimp into the air.

An **engine** moves the blimp through the air.

Blimps can only carry a few people.

What Are Some Special Aircraft?

ski

Seaplanes take off and land in water.

They float on two long **skis.**

basket

Hot-air balloons carry people in a basket.

Hot air lifts the balloon into the air.

Quiz

Do you know what kind of aircraft this is?

Can you find it in the book?

Look for the answer on page 24.

Picture Glossary

blade
pages 7, 16

hot-air balloon
page 21

skis
page 20

blimp
page 18

propeller
pages 5, 12, 14, 16

vehicle
page 4

engine
pages 5, 14, 16, 19

seaplane
page 20

Note to Parents and Teachers

Reading for information is an important part of a child's literacy development. Learning begins with a question about something. Help children think of themselves as investigators and researchers by encouraging their questions about the world around them. Each chapter in this book begins with a question. Read the question together. Talk about what you think the answer might be. Read the text to find out if your predictions were correct. Think of other questions you could ask about the topic, and discuss where you might find the answers. In this book, the picture glossary symbol for vehicle is an aircraft. Explain to children that a vehicle is something that can move people or things from one place to another. Some vehicles have motors, like cars, but others do not.

Index

Answer to quiz on page 22
This is a jet plane.